#THELASERCANON

THE LASER CANON

AN ASSOCIATIVE CANON
BASED ON CAT PHOTOS

NO AUTHOR

1st edition

This title is part of the series
NO AUTHOR.

© 2019 by Frohmann Verlag, Christiane Frohmann, Berlin. frohmann.orbanism.com

ISBN Paperback: 978-3-947047-49-9

Virginia Woolf

A ROOM OF ONE'S OWN

*

THE HOGARTH PRESS
LONDON, 1929

5

Oscar Wilde

The Picture of Dorian Gray

*

Ward, Lock and Co.
London, 1891

GEBRÜDER GRIMM

TISCHLEIN DECK DICH
(THE WISHING-TABLE)

*

IN: KINDER- UND HAUSMÄRCHEN
GEORG ANDREAS REIMER
BERLIN, 1812

Sylvia Plath

THE BELL JAR

*

Heinemann
Portsmouth, NH, 1963

11

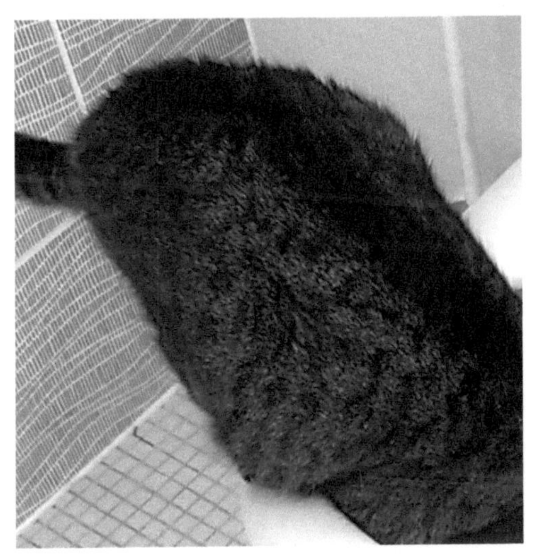

13

Chimamanda Ngozi Adichie

WE SHOULD ALL BE FEMINISTS

*

Fourth Estate
New York, NY, 2014

Victor Hugo

Notre-Dame de Paris
(The Hunchback of Notre-Dame)

*

Charles Gosselin
Paris, 1831

17

PRIDE AND PREJUDICE

*

T. EGERTON
WHITEHALL, 1813

19

GEORGE ORWELL

NINETEEN EIGHTY-FOUR

*

SECKER & WARBURG

LONDON, 1949

IMMANUEL KANT
KRITIK DER REINEN VERNUNFT
(CRITIQUE OF PURE REASON)

*

HARTKNOCH
RIGA, 1791

INGEBORG BACHMANN
MALINA

*

SUHRKAMP
FRANKFURT A. M., 1971

25

William Shakespeare

ROMEO AND JULIET

*

John Danter
London, 1597

27

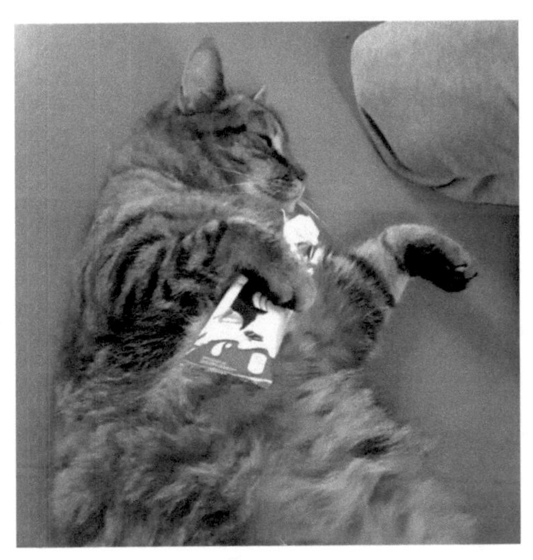

Roald Dahl

Charlie and the Chocolate Factory

*

Alfred A. Knopf
New York, NY, 1964

LA DAME AUX CAMÉLIAS
(CAMILLE)

*

LEBÈGUE

BRUXELLES, 1848

ON THE ROAD

*

VIKING PRESS
NEW YORK, NY, 1957

LEOPOLD VON SACHER-MASOCH

VENUS IM PELZ
(VENUS IN FURS)

*

COTTA
STUTTGART, 1870

André Breton

Manifeste du Surréalisme
(Surrealist Manifesto)

*

Editions du Sagittaire

Paris, 1924

37

CHARLOTTE BRONTË

JANE EYRE:
AN AUTOBIOGRAPHY

*

SMITH, ELDER & CO.
LONDON, 1847

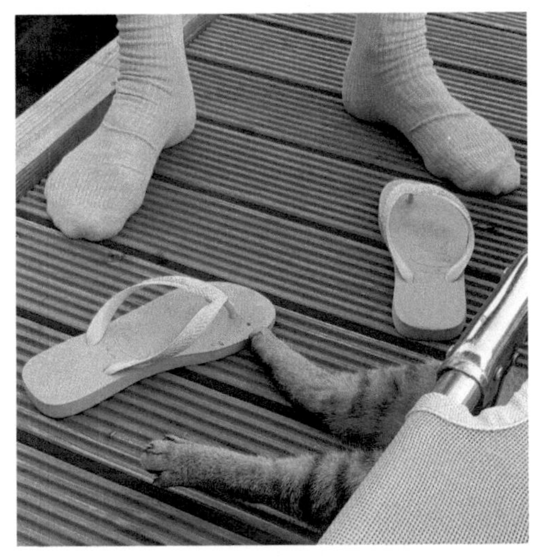

MARLENE STREERUWITZ
PARTYGIRL

*

FISCHER
FRANKFURT A. M., 2002

41

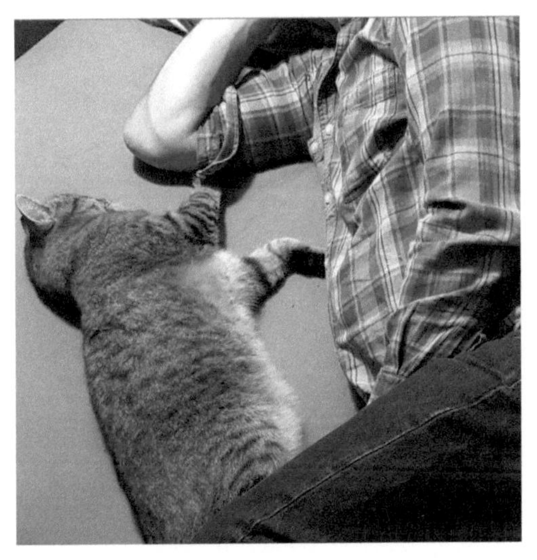

MARCEL PROUST

À LA RECHERCHE DU TEMPS PERDU

(IN SEARCH OF LOST TIME)

*

BERNARD GRASSET ET GALLIMARD

PARIS, 1913–1927

43

Hans Christian Andersen
PRINSESSEN PÅ ÆRTEN
(The Princess and the Pea)

*

C. A. Reitzel
København, 1837

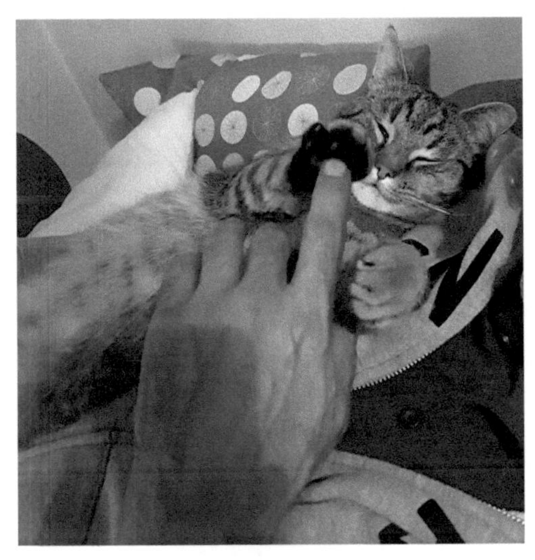

Jackie Thomae

BRÜDER
(BROTHERS)

*

HANSER
BERLIN, 2019

47

MICHEL FOUCAULT

SURVEILLER ET PUNIR: NAISSANCE DE LA PRISON

(DISCIPLINE AND PUNISH: THE BIRTH OF THE PRISON)

*

GALLIMARD

PARIS, 1975

49

Лев Николаевич Толстой

(Leo Tolstoy)

Война и мир

(War and Peace)

*

Русский вестник
Москва, 1868/69

ANN RADCLIFFE

THE MYSTERIES OF UDOLPHO

*

G. G. AND J. ROBINSON
LONDON, 1794

MARY WOLLSTONECRAFT SHELLEY

FRANKENSTEIN OR THE MODERN PROMETHEUS

*

LACKINGTON, HUGHES,
HARDING, MAVOR & JONES
LONDON, 1818

Giovanni Boccaccio

DECAMERON
(The Decameron)

*

Napoli, 1470

JOHANN WOLFGANG VON GOETHE

DIE LEIDEN DES JUNGEN WERTHERS

(THE SORROWS OF YOUNG WERTHER)

*

WEYGANDSCHE BUCHHANDLUNG

LEIPZIG 1774

59

Vor dem Gesetz
(Before the Law)

*

Kurt Wolff

Leipzig, 1915

N. K. JEMISIN
THE STONE SKY

*

ORBIT
LONDON, 2017

William Gibson

Neuromancer

*

Ace
New York, NY, 1984

65

SIMONE DE BEAUVOIR

LE DEUXIÈME SEXE

(THE SECOND SEX)

*

GALLIMARD

PARIS, 1949

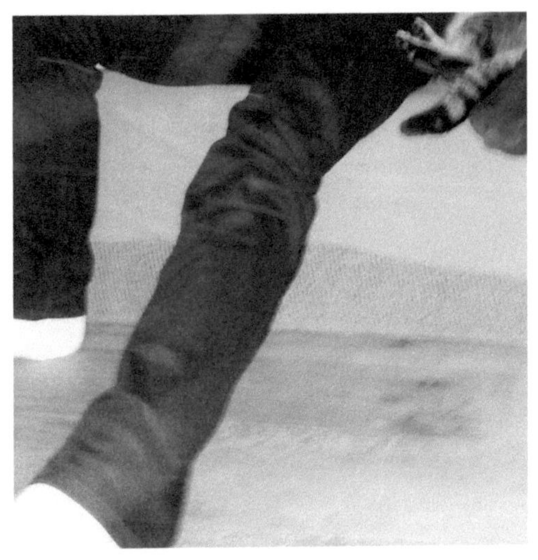

John Kennedy Toole

A Confederacy of Dunces

*

Louisiana State University Press
Baton Rouge, Louisiana, 1980

69

ANNIE ERNAUX

UNE FEMME
(A WOMAN'S STORY)

*

GALLIMARD

PARIS, 1988

71

MARGARET ATWOOD
THE HANDMAID'S TALE

*

MCCLELLAND & STEWART
TORONTO, ONTARIO, 1985

73

LASER IS A TEN YEAR OLD HOUSE CAT
WHO LIVES IN BERLIN.

THE CANON PRESENTED IN THIS BOOK IS
COMPLETELY ARBITRARY. BUT MOST OF
THE BOOKS ARE QUITE GOOD.

HTTPS://ORBANISM.COM/FROHMANN